The Heart of a Leader

KEN BLANCHARD

Co-author

The One Minute Manager

HONOR HB BOOKS

Inspiration and Motivation for the Seasons of Life

COOK COMMUNICATIONS MINISTRIES
Colorado Springs, Colorado • Paris, Ontario
KINGSWAY COMMUNICATIONS LTD
Eastbourne, England

Honor Books® is an imprint of
Cook Communications Ministries, Colorado Springs, CO 80918
Cook Communications, Paris, Ontario
Kingsway Communications, Eastbourne, England

The Heart of a Leader
© 1999 by The Blanchard Family Partner
The Ken Blanchard Companies
125 State Place
Escondido, California 92029-1398

Printed in India

13 14 15 16 17 Printing/Year 09 08 07 06 05

ISBN: 1-56292-488-5

Introduction

When I was in high school, we had a football coach who loved motivational sayings. They covered the walls of our locker room. Sayings like, "When the going gets tough, the tough get going" and "Quitters never win and winners never quit" were imprinted in my mind. As a result, when I started teaching and writing in the field of leadership and management, I used sayings to help people remember key points.

That's why I was thrilled when the Honor Books folks asked me to write a book that included my favorite sayings. With the help of long-time friend and writing colleague Jim Ballard and the fabulous editing of Rebecca Currington from Honor Books, *The Heart of a Leader* became a reality.

I hope the sayings in this book and my comments will give you the business smarts you need to become an effective leader and manager. I hope you will also come to realize the best way to achieve high performance and remarkable results is with a caring "business heart."

God bless!

Ken Blanchard

The key to developing people is to catch them doing something right.

Ken Blanchard and Spencer Johnson
The One Minute Manager®

Catching people doing things right is a powerful management concept. Unfortunately, most leaders have a genius for catching people doing things wrong. I always recommend that leaders spend at least an hour a week wandering around their operation catching people doing things right.

But I remind them, effective praising must be specific. Just walking around saying, "Thanks for everything" is meaningless. If you say, "Great job" to a poor performer and, "Great job" to a good performer, you sound ridiculous to the poor performer and you "demotivate" the good performer.

Catching people doing things right provides satisfaction and motivates good performance. But remember, give praise immediately, make it specific, and finally, encourage people to keep up the good work. This principle can also help you shine at home. It's a marvelous way to interact with and affirm the people in your life.

People
who produce
good results
feel good
about
themselves.

Ken Blanchard and Robert Lorber
Putting the One Minute Manager® to Work

In *The One Minute Manager,* Spencer Johnson and I wrote "People who feel good about themselves produce good results." After the book came out, I realized I was emphasizing the "old" human relations game—trying to make people feel good first and then hoping they would produce good results. Hence the change in emphasis when we wrote *Putting the One Minute Manager® to Work.*

These days, everything our company does is focused on helping people produce good results. When people produce good results, they feel good about themselves because they know they have done a good job, and they have something to show for their effort.

An effective leader will make it a priority to help his or her people produce good results in two ways:

1) Make sure people know what their goals are, and
2) Do everything possible to support, encourage, and coach them to accomplish those goals.

Your role as a leader is even more important than you might imagine. You have the power to help people become winners.

Don't wait until people do things exactly right before you praise them.

Ken Blanchard and Spencer Johnson
The One Minute Manager®

8

Many well-intentioned leaders wait to praise their people until they do things exactly right—complete the project or accomplish the goal. The problem here is that they could wait forever. You see, "exactly right" behavior is made up of a whole series of approximately right behaviors. It makes more sense to praise progress—it's a moving target.

Can you imagine standing a child up and saying, "Walk," and when he falls down, you say, "I told you to walk!" and then spank him. Of course not. You stand the child up and he wobbles a bit. You shout, "You stood!" and shower him with hugs and kisses. The next day, he wobbles a step and you are all over him with praise. Gradually, the child gains confidence until he finally walks. It's the same with adults. Catch them doing things right—and in the beginning, approximately right is fine.

Feedback
is the
breakfast
of
champions.

Rick Tate

In my travels, I see a lot of unmotivated people at work, but I've never seen an unmotivated person after work. When 5 o'clock rolls around, they race from the office to play golf or tennis, coach Little League, etc. People are motivated to do things that provide them with feedback on results. Feedback is important to people. We all want to know how well we're doing. That's why it is essential for an effective performance review system to provide ongoing feedback.

Too often managers save up negative information and unload it all at once over a minor incident or during the annual performance review session. Others "whitewash" performance review and act like everything is okay when it really isn't. When people are attacked or not dealt with truthfully, they lose respect for their organization and pride in their work.

I firmly believe that providing feedback is the most cost-effective strategy for improving performance and instilling satisfaction. It can be done quickly, it costs nothing, and it can turn people around fast.

No one can make you feel inferior without your permission.

Eleanor Roosevelt

I go out into the world every day with the attitude that my "okayness" is not up for grabs. I firmly believe that "God did not make junk." This doesn't mean I don't have areas of my life that need improvement—just that at my basic core, I'm okay.

I *choose* to feel good about myself. That way I am more open to learning. If people give me negative feedback or criticize something I do, I don't interpret what they are saying as meaning that I am a "bad" person. The belief that I control my own self-esteem permits me to listen to and hear their feedback in a nondefensive way—looking to see if there is something I can learn.

Norman Vincent Peale taught me that we have two choices every day: We can feel good about ourselves, or we can feel lousy about ourselves. Why would anyone choose the latter?

None of us is as smart as all of us.

Ken Blanchard, Don Carew,
and Eunice Parisi-Carew
*The One Minute Manager® Builds
High Performing Teams*

This quote has become the guiding principle of our team-building work in organizations. When I first caught the truth of this statement, it made me relax tremendously, as a leader. I realized that I didn't have to be the only bright person in the group. In fact, admitting my vulnerability allowed me to ask for help. I experienced an example of this while working with a large Southern manufacturing plant.

The president was baffled over a 200 percent turnover in one of the plant's major hourly positions. I asked to speak to the workers in the affected area, knowing they would be the key to finding an answer.

They told me, "It's hot as the devil down here. We're so exhausted by the end of the day that we don't have energy to do anything else. So if we can get another job, we do." I reported my findings to the president, they fixed the cooling system, and turnover dropped to around 10 percent. I'm convinced that any problem can be solved if we involve the resources we have gathered around us.

Things *not* worth doing are not worth doing well.

Ken Blanchard, William Oncken, and Hal Burrows
The One Minute Manager®
Meets the Monkey

William Oncken Jr., originator of the "Monkey-on-the-back" concept, used to say this all the time. For years, time-management experts taught efficiency in all things; then Oncken and others realized that it didn't make sense for people to be efficient at doing what they shouldn't be doing in the first place.

Today people are often busy doing what seems to be extremely urgent but really isn't. They spend a great deal of time moving paper, rather than listening to their people or their customers. An effective leader must step back, look at the big picture, and make sure the important things are not pushed out of the way by the urgent needs of the moment.

If your people and customers are important, then you will spend part of every day making them feel that way. Evaluate each day by asking, "Have I done what is really important today?"

Success
is not forever
and failure
isn't fatal.

Ken Blanchard and Don Shula
Everyone's a Coach

This was Don Shula's favorite quote when he was head coach of the Miami Dolphins. It drove a great deal of his behavior during his long and distinguished career as the "winningest" coach in the history of the NFL.

Don had a twenty-four hour rule. He allowed himself, his coaches, and his players a maximum of twenty-four hours after a football game to celebrate a victory or bemoan a defeat. During that time, they were encouraged to experience the thrill of victory or the agony of defeat as deeply as possible. Once the twenty-four hour deadline had passed, they put it behind them and focused their energies on preparing for the next opponent. This is a principle well worth noting.

Don't get a big head when you win or get too down in the dumps when you lose. Keep things in perspective. Success is not forever, and failure isn't fatal.

When you
stop
learning,
you stop
growing.

When I first met Norman Vincent Peale, he was 86 years old. What amazed me about him more than anything was that he was excited about every single day. Why? He never knew what he might learn that day. He often said, "When I stop learning, I might as well lie down because I will be dead." He was learning right up until his death a few years ago on Christmas Eve, at age 95.

Learning is more important today than ever before. In the past, if a person was loyal and worked hard, his or her job was secure. Today, the skills you bring to the party constitute the only available form of job security. People who are continually learning and upgrading their skills increase their value in their specific organization and the job market in general.

The only three things we can count on are death, taxes, and change. Since organizations are being bombarded with change, you would be wise to make learning a top priority and constantly strive to adapt to new circumstances.

In life,
what you resist,
persists.

Werner Erhard

If something is bothering you and you don't deal with it, you are gunnysacking your feelings—holding them inside. This can backfire later when you find yourself "dumping" in an inappropriate way and at exactly the wrong moment. It is also true that if you will deal with what is bothering you, the problem often disappears in the very process. Have you ever said, "I'm glad I got that off my mind"?

I worked for several divisions of AT&T during the transition to seven sister companies. Though top leadership emphasized the benefits of the change, associates were not being encouraged to deal with their feelings. I set up venting sessions where they could "mourn" their personal losses as companies were restructured. The associates were urged to share their feelings of loss regarding status, lifetime employment, etc. They soon became open to hearing the benefits of the changes for the first time and move forward with their lives and careers.

What you resist, persists. Until you deal with your feelings, you will be stuck with them.

Don't work harder— work smarter.

This saying is common sense but not common practice. Most people still think there is a direct relationship between the amount of work they do and success—the more time you put in, the more successful you will be. One successful entrepreneur when asked to speak to a group of college students about what it took to be successful said, "This will be the shortest speech in history because it's easy to be successful. All you have to do is work half a day. You can work the first twelve hours or the second."

While successful people do work hard, they think before they act. They are proactive, not just reactive. Most people mentally have a sign on their desk that reads: *Don't just sit there, do something!* The best advice I ever received was to redo the sign to read: *Don't just do something, sit there!*

If you don't take time out to think, strategize, and prioritize, you will work a whole lot harder, without enjoying the benefits of a job smartly done.

Nice guys
may appear
to finish last,
but usually
they are running
in a different race.

Ken Blanchard and Norman Vincent Peale
The Power of Ethical Management

People today want what they want, and they want it right now. A negative side effect of such impatience is poor decision-making. Patience helps us to realize that if we do what is right—even if it costs us in the short run—it will pay off in the long run.

Norman Vincent Peale told a story about a nice guy who eventually won. He was fired as the art director of a magazine because he refused to work on a project that included what he considered to be pornographic material. He had a difficult time finding another job, and even his kids had to get jobs after school to help out.

Finally, almost a year later, he was offered a great job—even better than the one he had lost. Ironically, he clinched the new job as a result of his old boss's recommendation! He had earned his boss's respect. His patience paid off, because he was running in a different race.

In
managing people
it is easier
to loosen up
than
tighten up.

Ken Blanchard, Patricia Zigarmi,
and Drea Zigarmi
Leadership and the One Minute Manager®

28

If you are not sure how much direction people need to do a task, it's always better to *oversupervise* than *undersupervise* in the beginning. Why? Because if you find your people are better than you thought, and you loosen up, they will like you and respond in a positive way. It also helps as you seek to communicate your growing respect for the quality of work your people are producing.

If on the other hand, you start off *undersupervising* your people and later discover their skills are not as good as you anticipated, you then have a sticky situation. Even when it is appropriate to correct or redirect their work, you may find they perceive your efforts as undue criticism, micro-managing, or even persecution. After all, they aren't doing anything differently so why are you suddenly bent on changing things. Resentment grows.

It's easier to start off tough and then be nice than start off nice and then get tough. It's easier to loosen up than tighten up.

Anything
worth doing does
not have to be
done perfectly—
at first.

Managers should recognize that good performance, both their own and others, is a journey, not a destination. Everyone learns by doing. It takes time and practice to achieve specific goals.

For example, the managers who attend my training seminars often get very excited by some of the concepts they learn. They return to their organizations all fired up about using a new idea or approach. However, when people don't respond immediately as anticipated, they often become discouraged and abandon the concept, deciding that it doesn't work.

It's counterproductive to be too hard on yourself. Don't expect instant perfection. While self-criticism is healthy, it should not be destructive. It's unfair to be hard on yourself the first time you attempt something new. It is also unfair to expect such an unrealistic standard from others. It's not necessary to do everything exactly right the first time.

What
motivates people
is what
motivates
people.

Motivation is a difficult concept for most leaders. Many assume that money, prizes, or special vacations are high-grade motivators. In reality, what motivates one person may not motivate another.

Suppose you have two excellent people. You would like to reward one with a raise in pay, but money, it turns out, is not an issue with this person since his or her spouse has a good job that provides a nice second income. He or she may see increased responsibility as an appropriate reward. On the other hand, you would like to reward the second person with more responsibility, but his or her spouse's unexpected illness has created big medical bills. For this person, money is a greater motivator than increased responsibility.

How do you know what motivation works with what employees? Ask! Try something like, "If you perform well, what reward or recognition could you receive that would make you want to continue to perform at a high level?" It pays to ask this important question.

Life
is
all about
getting A's.

During my ten years of college teaching, I sometimes got in trouble with other faculty members because I always gave out the final examination questions on the first day of class. When my colleagues asked why, I would reply, "Because I plan to spend the semester teaching them the answers so when it comes time for the final, everyone will get an 'A.'"

My teaching example parallels the three parts of an effective review system: 1) *performance planning* when goals and objectives are set, 2) *day-to-day coaching* when on-going feedback is given, and 3) *performance evaluation* when overall performance is determined.

In business, communicating performance objectives —giving people the final exam questions ahead of time—is the perfect way to ensure that everyone is working from the same sheet of music and headed in the right direction. Once goals are clear, leaders should wander around and "teach people the answers" so when they get to the final exam they get an "A." After all, that's what life is all about!

Create
Raving Fans®;
satisfied customers
are not
good enough.

Ken Blanchard and Sheldon Bowles
Raving Fans®

What are raving fan® customers? These are customers who are so happy about the way you treated them that they want to brag about you. In essence, they become part of your sales force.

There is a lot of competition out there. If you don't take care of your customers, somebody else is ready to take your place. Let's face it, you may not get a second chance. In fact, alienating customers can earn you a reputation for *non*-service that can stymie the toughest sales team and most savvy advertising campaign.

Differentiate yourself from your competition by teaching your sales force and customer-service representatives—everyone who comes in contact with your public—to develop "raving fan" customers. Going the "extra mile" for the people who write your checks will pay off.

If you want
to know why
your people
are not
performing well,
step up to
the mirror
and take a peek.

From my point of view, one of the worst concepts in the history of leadership theory is the "Peter Principle." According to the Peter Principle, people in organizations tend to rise to their level of incompetence. In other words, they keep getting promoted until they become a failure. I think this concept lets managers off the hook.

Good leaders are committed to helping their people win. When someone fails, they accept responsibility for that failure. I think anytime you fire someone who works for you or anytime you're looking for a place to hide someone who works for you (Lawrence Peter called this "a lateral arabesque"), step up to a mirror and take a peek. In most cases, the biggest cause of the problem is looking you in the eyes.

The main job of a leader is to help his or her people succeed in accomplishing their goals. And when people accomplish their goals and win, everyone wins.

Managing
only for profit is
like playing tennis
with your eye
on the scoreboard
and not on
the ball.

Ichek Adizes

The best definition of profit I ever heard is that profit is the applause you get for satisfying your customers and creating a motivating environment for your people. Too bad Wall Street doesn't embrace that definition. The problem is that too many people act like the *only* reason to stay in business is to make money. Their eyes are on the scoreboard rather than the ball!

Successful organizations today have a triple bottom line—very much like a three-legged stool. The three legs of the stool are Raving Fan® customers, gung ho employees, and financial strength. All three legs have to be strong for the stool to stand. If you focus on only one leg, the stool will fall. Even if you focus on two legs, but forget the third, the stool will fall.

If you focus just on financial success and forget your employees and your customers, eventually, your financial success will decline.

If you want
your people
to be responsible,
be responsive
to their needs.

The traditional hierarchy is okay for goal setting. People look to the head of their department and to the top of the organization for direction. But once goals are clear, the pyramid should in essence be turned upside down. This way the customers are at the top of the hierarchy, followed by the customer contact people, while the president and the chairman of the board are at the bottom.

When this philosophy is implemented, your role as a leader changes from being "responsible" to being "responsive." Your job becomes to work *with* your people rather than having them work *for* you. Being responsive to your people's needs sets them free to be responsible (able to respond) for getting the job done.

Make your people responsible for doing high-quality work by responding to their needs and supporting them. That places the responsibility at the appropriate level—with the people who do the work.

It's
more important
as a manager
to be respected
than to be
popular.

Ken Blanchard and Don Shula
Everyone's a Coach

Think back to a leader you had—a parent, teacher, coach or boss who got great performance from you. More than likely, this was a leader who combined *tough* and *nice.* You knew that person cared about you, but that he or she would not let up on you in the quest for excellence.

If you, as a leader, demand that your people add value to the organization through their work, you must fulfill your end of the bargain by telling the truth and keeping work standards high. This often means sacrificing popularity in your endeavor to do the right thing.

Are you willing to push your people—whether it's a group of middle managers or a Cub Scout pack—beyond their comfort zone in order to achieve excellence? They might not like what you ask of them, but they will remember you as a leader they respected.

People
with humility
don't think
less of themselves,
they just think of
themselves less.

Ken Blanchard and Norman Vincent Peale
The Power of Ethical Management

A friend of mine jokes about his latest book, *Humility and How I Attained It*. It reminds me of what I call the greatest addiction in the world today—the human ego.

Leaders who fall victim to this addiction want to be center stage. They often are threatened by the successes of others, so they fail to develop and use people's talents or catch them doing something right. They want to be the best—"the fairest of them all."

A great rule for doing business today is: Think more about your people, and they will think more of themselves. And don't act like you are perfect. Leaders need to come from behind their curtains of infallibility, power, and control, and let their "very good" side—their humanity—be revealed. Folks like to be around a person who is willing to admit his or her vulnerability, asks for ideas, and can let others be in the spotlight.

Never!
Never!
Never!
Never!
Give Up!

Winston Churchill

In his later years, Winston Churchill gave a speech at the English prep school he attended as a boy. The headmaster told the boys, "This is an historic moment. Winston Churchill is the greatest speaker of the English language. Write down everything he says. He will make an unforgettable speech."

When Churchill walked out to give his speech, he peered over the top of his glasses and said: "Never! Never! Never! Never! Give up!" With that, he sat down. Many students were disappointed, but the headmaster felt this might have been one of Churchill's greatest speeches. If one quality epitomized Winston Churchill, it was persistence. He never gave up. It was that attitude that inspired England in World War II to continue fighting when others might have surrendered.

Persistence means sticking to your guns. It's keeping your commitment and making your actions consistent with your word. It's all about "walking your talk."

Trying
is just a noisy
way of
not
doing
something.

I learned from author and consultant Art Turock that we need to make a distinction between being interested and being committed. When you are "interested" in doing something, you only do it when it's convenient, but when you are "committed," you follow through no matter what—no excuses!

Many people are interested rather than committed. They talk about *trying* to do something, rather than actually doing it. They make lots of noise, but fail to follow up. An interested exerciser wakes up in the morning to rain and says, "I think I'll exercise tomorrow." A committed exerciser wakes up to rain and says, "I better exercise inside."

When a person is committed to doing something, he or she will find ways to suppress rationalization. Even when it is inconvenient, such a person will keep his or her commitment. Persistence in life is characterized by this mental and behavioral toughness.

Good thoughts
in your head
not delivered
mean
"squat."

There are three responses people can receive from leadership concerning their performance—positive, negative, or no response at all. Only one response of the three tends to increase good performance—the positive one. And yet, the major leadership style used today is "leave alone—zap!"

A person who does something correctly and receives a positive response will most likely continue that desired behavior in the future. By the same token, a person who receives a negative response for doing something wrong will most likely not repeat the behavior. But what if someone does something correctly and receives no response at all? The behavior may continue for awhile, but eventually it will decline. Why? Because no one seems to care.

Many leaders notice their people doing things right and think well of them. Unfortunately, they do not always put those positive thoughts into words. As a result, this good performance gets no response. If you want to get and maintain good performance, you must let your people know you notice and care about the things they do right. Share your good thoughts.

You may fool the
whole world down
the pathway of life
    and get pats on your
back as you pass,
    but your final reward will
be heartaches and tears
    if you've cheated
the man in the glass.

Dale Wimbrow

This is the closing verse of a poem given to Norman Vincent Peale by Lowell Thomas one day after hearing one of Norman's sermons. He said, "Frankly, if you had read this poem, your talk would have been much better." Obviously Dr. Peale agreed, because he kept a copy of the poem in his wallet and referred to it frequently.

While the message is loud and clear, you might ask, "But don't some people do the wrong thing and then rationalize what they've done?" Yes, people do that, but if they take a good hard look at themselves, down deep they know they have done wrong.

You can't go against your image of yourself and what you think is right without feeling bad. It's counter to your purpose—the picture you have of yourself as an ethical person. A clear purpose is the foundation upon which sound, ethical behavior is built.

Sometimes
when the
numbers look
right
the decision
is still
wrong!

Ken Blanchard and Norman Vincent Peale
The Power of Ethical Management

Good business requires more than simply calculating which choice will make the most money. It requires developing some way to step back from things and put them in perspective.

I know a leader who uses a three-step approach when faced with a serious problem or an important decision. *First,* he calls his team together for *information gathering.* Each person is asked to contribute, until as much information as possible has been amassed about the problem or decision. *Second,* the group works together to word what he calls the *right question.* If answered, this question should yield the best possible solution. *Third,* he asks each person to sit quietly for ten minutes and look for the answer within. He calls this *inward listening.*

My friend has been amazed by the clarity of thought and agreement that emerges from these sessions. If you don't find creative ways like this to get things in perspective, you will continue to be driven only by the bottom line.

Love
is being able to
say you're
sorry.

E ven if you didn't read the book *Love Story* or see the movie, I'll bet you can recall this saying that became famous from Eric Segal's story: "Love is never having to say you're sorry." People loved that saying, but I think it's awful, especially for leaders. I think it should read: "Love is being able to say you're sorry." Yet, saying "I'm sorry" is tough on the ego. Leaders are often reluctant to admit they are wrong and ask forgiveness.

Some years ago, I received a letter from a top manager at Honeywell who suggested that the forth secret of *The One Minute Manager*® should be the "One Minute Apology." That resonated with me, because my mother always said, "There are two statements that people don't use enough that could change the world: "thank you" and "I'm sorry." The "One Minute Praising" covered "thank you," but we didn't have anything that corresponded to "I'm sorry."

If as a leader you can give up being right and learn to apologize for your mistakes, your organization will be a lot better place for people to work. Thanks, Mom.

Good religion
is like
good football;
it isn't talk,
it's action.

Ken Blanchard and Don Shula
Everyone's a Coach

People in general and especially in the business world are looking for leaders whose faith works for them on a day-to-day basis. Why? Because in business today, your opponents are multiplied, your risks are increased, and the number of factors that could spell success or failure are proliferating constantly.

To win this new business game, your faith must be the genuine article. You must be able to rely on intuition—that calm inner voice that tells you what to do. At the same time, you must be relentless in your pursuit of opportunity. This paradoxical equilibrium between trusting in your own way as you approach danger and calmly discerning the outward signals is actually very close to what we call "faith."

Traditionally, business and religion have been seen as opposite approaches. That day is over. The demands of business and of life are too great. Thank God!

Take
what you do
seriously
but
yourself
lightly.

Ken Blanchard and Terry Waghorn
Mission Possible

A tendency toward grimness and seriousness can stifle an organization's environment and limit its creativity. You can tell right away when you visit a company where no one is having any fun—people look like they are running around with tight underwear on. They are longing to lighten up, but they have no permission.

These days, leaders and managers are being offered courses in humor. These classes don't teach the art of telling a good joke; they are aimed at helping people contact something they already have inside—their sense of humor. Increasing someone's natural ability to see the funny or absurd side of a situation will have a direct bearing on his or her effectiveness with others.

Today's leaders must relearn the value of a smile or they will be unable to fire up the ability of their people to find real enjoyment in their work. So start thinking smiles until you become a smile millionaire. People will be glad to see you coming.

The trouble
with being in
a rat race
is that even if
you win the race,
you're still a rat.

Lily Tomlin

We all have two selves—an inner self that is thoughtful, reflective, and a good listener; and an outer, task-oriented self. Our inner self is focused on connecting with people and finding significance in life; while our outer, task-oriented self is focused on achieving and often too busy to learn.

To avoid the rat race and stay on course, we must honor our inner selves. The only way to do that is to seek out times of solitude when we can be alone with the voice that says, "You are a loved and valuable person."

Solitude is hard to find. Therefore, I recommend that people enter their day slowly by engaging in an activity that is intrinsically valuable and noncompetitive such as prayer, meditation, reflective reading, or certain kinds of exercise. Walking, running, swimming, biking, and other activities that allow you to reflect while you are doing them are perfect.

Think Big!
Act Big!
Be Big!

Norman Vincent Peale

At his ninetieth birthday party, Norman Vincent Peale, the great minister of positive thinking, shared a story about a man he met on a plane. The man looked worried so Norman decided to engage him in conversation. "What's wrong?" he asked. After some coaxing, the man shared that he had just received a promotion, but had doubts about whether he had what it would take to handle the job.

"Yes you do!" stated Dr. Peale. "How do you know?" the man replied. Dr. Peale answered, "You do if you *think* you do." Then he encouraged the man to start each day by chanting, *"Think big! Act big! Be big!"* By the time they landed, the man was in a different frame of mind.

Be your own best friend and believe in yourself. Don't wait for someone to do it for you. Cheer yourself on. Write your own pep talk. It works.

Real communication happens when people feel safe.

R eal communication is a product of *trust.* However, most of the performance review and evaluation systems used in organizations today create *mistrust.* They are based on a normal distribution mentality that insists there must always be winners and losers. That has never made sense to me.

No organization makes a habit of hiring losers! You either hire winners (people you already know are good performers) or potential winners (people you think can become good performers). So why would you ever sort your people out into a normal distribution? Your job is to bring out their magnificence.

Find ways to convince your people that you see them all as either winners or potential winners and you *mean them no harm.* When you do, you will find that communication within your organization is greatly enhanced.

All good performance starts with clear goals.

The reason Spencer Johnson and I made "One Minute Goal Setting" the first secret of *The One Minute Manager®* is that we thought the Cheshire Cat was right. Do you remember the story?

Alice was puzzled. As she searched for a way out of Wonderland, she came to a fork in the road. "Which road should I take?" she asked the Cheshire Cat. "Where are you going?" the cat responded. *Alice said she didn't know.* The smiling cat gave her this reply, "If you don't know where you're going, any road will get you there."

An important way to motivate your people is to make sure they know where they are going. See that each person's goals are clearly defined and he or she knows what good performance looks like. This will give them a clear focus for their energy and put them on the road to becoming high performing, empowered producers.

Different strokes for different folks.

Ken Blanchard, Patricia Zigarmi,
and Drea Zigarmi
Leadership and
The One Minute Manager®

For years, people thought that the best leadership style was a "participative" style, which prescribed listening to your people and involving them in decision making. Autocratic leadership, where the leader took control and told people what to do, was considered inappropriate.

In the 1960s, my friend Paul Hersey and I questioned those assumptions. The problem we found was that asking inexperienced members of a team to participate in decision-making amounted to "pooling ignorance." Some people need a "directive" leadership style until their knowledge and skills mature. Our response was to develop a concept called Situational Leadership®, which can be summed up in the statement, "Different strokes for different folks."

So what is the best leadership style? The one that matches the developmental needs of the person with whom you're working.

Different strokes
for
the same folks.

Ken Blanchard, Patricia Zigarmi,
and Drea Zigarmi
Leadership and
The One Minute Manager®

Situational Leadership® II identifies four development levels people go through as they move from dependence to independence in doing a task.

These include the Enthusiastic Beginner (excited but has little knowledge), the Disillusioned Learner (learning the task was tougher than he or she thought), the Capable but Cautious Performer (knows how to do it but is nervous about doing it on his or her own), and the Self-Reliant Achiever (confident, motivated, and has the necessary skills).

The point is that no individual is at any *one* stage in all the tasks he or she performs. Consequently, the same person may need different leadership styles (different strokes) for various tasks. For example, when I was a college professor, I loved to teach and write. Those were tasks I performed well and without supervision. However, when it came to administrative matters like managing my budget and filling out reports, I was a "Disillusioned Learner" at best. Sometimes it takes different strokes for the same folks.

If God had
wanted us to talk
more than listen,
He would have
given us two
mouths rather
than two ears.

Ken Blanchard
We Are the Beloved

When you ask people about the best leader they ever had, one quality is always mentioned—they are good listeners. They have learned to "sort by others." When someone says, "It's a beautiful day," they respond by keeping the focus on the speaker. For example, "Sounds like you're pretty happy today." Poor listeners "sort by self." If you express a concern you have, they will express a concern *they* have.

Our senior consulting partner, Laurie Hawkins, is a wonderful listener. Clients tell me, "I had the greatest dinner with Laurie recently. He's a wonderful person." When I ask what they know about Laurie—whether he's married, has kids, etc., they seldom know. They loved being with Laurie because he kept the conversation focused on them.

Test the power of listening for yourself by taking time to listen and focus on others.

Life is what
happens to you
while you're
planning on doing
something else.

John Lennon

Observing successful people over the years, I've noticed that they don't let disappointments stop them. When one door closes, they look for another to open.

I went off to Cornell University intent on getting my degree and becoming a highly paid salesperson. All the vocational preference tests verified that as my best career choice. I applied for a summer sales internship and made the finals, but after extensive interviews, I failed to get the job. At the time, I was serving as a dormitory counselor, so someone encouraged me to get my doctorate and become a dean of students. With doctoral degree in hand, I applied for many good jobs but I was turned down because of a lack of experience. Undeterred, I set my sights on becoming a faculty member, but I was told that would be impossible because my writing wasn't academic enough.

"So how," you might ask, "did you become a writer and teacher?" That's a long story, but along the way I learned to live by this rule: Keep your head up and look for the next opportunity.

Without vision the people perish.

Proverbs 29:18 (paraphrased)

Leaders today must have a strong vision and positive beliefs that support that vision. If they don't, their people will not only lose, they'll be lost. When difficulties arise, their minds will not be equal to the challenge.

A clear vision is really just a picture of how things would be if everything were running as planned. The most powerful dream a leader can have is a vision of perfection. Dreams lift us up. If we really believe them, we start acting as if they are already true. That kind of enthusiasm is contagious.

All great companies and teams have a visionary leader at the helm, who is always pointing at the kind of organization they're going to be. People have a need to follow this type of leader. It inspires them and keeps them on track when difficulties arise.

If you don't seek perfection, you can never reach excellence.

Ken Blanchard and Don Shula
Everyone's a Coach

The level of people's expectations has a great deal to do with the results they achieve. Don Shula's vision of perfection for the football team he coached was to win every game. Was that possible? No, but the 1972 Miami Dolphins did it for a season—establishing a level of perfection that no other NFL team has ever matched.

Don's philosophy is that if you're shooting at a target, you're better off aiming at the bull's-eye because if you miss it, the chances are high you'll still be on the target. On the other hand, if you aim just for the target and miss, you're nowhere.

If Shula's goal had been just to win more games than he lost, do you think he would have recorded the only perfect season on record and become the winningest coach in NFL history? Personally, I don't think so.

People without
information cannot
act responsibly.
People with
information are
compelled to act
responsibly.

Ken Blanchard, John P. Carlos, Alan Randolph
Empowerment Takes More Than a Minute

Many organizations don't seem to trust their people. For example, have you ever written a check for groceries at the supermarket? The cashier verifies your ID, writes the numbers on the check, and then you both wait around while the cashier calls the manager or assistant manager to come over and give his or her approval.

When that happens, doesn't this process leave you with the impression that the store doesn't trust its cashiers, and the only employees who have brains are the managers?

I wonder what would happen if those cashiers were given all the detailed information about the impact of bad checks on the business and then entrusted with check approval power? Research confirms that the result would be fewer bounced checks. In addition, self-esteem rises and customer service is improved. When you give people information and the chance to act responsibly, they usually come through.

A river
without banks
is
a large puddle.

Ken Blanchard, John P. Carlos,
Alan Randolph
*Empowerment Takes More
Than a Minute*

Start your people on a journey to the land of empowerment, but don't forget that they need boundaries. If you cut them loose without any direction, they will get lost and revert back to their old unempowered habits. Like the banks of a river, boundaries have the ability to channel energy in the right direction. If you take away the boundaries, your people will lose their momentum and direction.

Boundaries that create autonomy include: 1) Purpose—what does your company do? 2) Values—what are your company's operational guidelines? 3) Goals—where is your company headed? 4) Roles—who does what? 5) Structure—how is your company organized?

Don't send your people off on their own with no experience and then punish them when they make mistakes. Establish clear boundaries that will free them to make decisions, take initiative, act like owners, and stay on track.

Your game
is only
as good as
your practice.

Ken Blanchard and Don Shula
Everyone's a Coach

Coach Don Shula believed in "practice perfection." He often quoted Paul Brown, the legendary coach of the Cleveland Browns, who said, "Football is a game of errors. The team that makes the fewest errors in a game usually wins."

Companies need to approach the performance of their people with the same kind of attention to quality, but as I travel around looking at organizations, I rarely find this emphasis on "practice perfection." Far more often, companies hire highly competent people, get them started, and then leave them to struggle on their own.

No individual or team can reach "practice perfection" alone. It takes ferocious concentration and unyielding commitment to continuous improvement. That means day-to-day coaching—setting clear goals, letting people perform, observing, and then praising progress or redirecting efforts. Most managers miss the "observe" step. They give directions, but they don't stick around to redirect their people or catch them doing something right. "You can't coach from the press box," Shula used to say, "you have to be on the field."

All empowerment
exists in the
present moment.

Consider moments when you were at your best, and you will find that you were right there in the moment, fully and completely present. If you dwell only on "what was" or "what will be," you will miss the power of "what is."

Spencer Johnson, co-author of *The One Minute Manager*®, talks about this important truth in his brilliant parable, *The Precious Present.* In the story, an older man's wisdom launches a young boy on a lifelong search for the "Precious Present." Finally, he discovers what the old man was trying to tell him: To learn from the past is good, but to live there is a waste. To plan for the future is good, but to live there is a waste. You are happiest and most productive in life when you are living in the present.

All highly effective leaders have learned to respect the power of the present. They have discovered that analyzing the past and planning the future is not enough; they must also nurture the present and celebrate its victories.

We are not
human beings
having a spiritual
experience.
We are
spiritual beings
having a human
experience.

It becomes clearer to me all the time that leaders today have to start being cheerleaders, supporters, and encouragers, rather than judges, critics, and evaluators. Unfortunately, it's almost impossible for people to play these new roles if they don't feel good about themselves.

I believe personally that the quickest and most powerful way for individuals to significantly enhance their self-esteem and become a more loving and accepting person is by having a "spiritual awakening."

Suppose that we accepted the fact that we have the unconditional love of God our Father—that we can't achieve enough, sell enough, build enough, or own enough to merit more love—we have all the love there is. Would knowing this truth make us better cheerleaders, supporters, and encouragers for our people? I think so. When you discover that you are a spiritual being having a human experience, you realize that everyone else is too.

You get from people what you expect.

Whenever I talk about the power of catching people doing things right, I hear, "Yeah right. You don't know Harry!" Do you have a "Harry" in your life? If so, perhaps you should take a look at your expectations for that person and see if he or she isn't currently living *down* to them.

It's all in what you notice. When you judge someone, it impairs your ability to see him or her clearly. It is as if a filter is screening out everything about that person except what fits your assessment. Fight through your filter and catch your "Harry" doing something right. This will not be easy, but if you persevere, you will notice that your behavior, even your attitude or degree of acceptance toward "Harry" is changing.

Try it and see what happens. Then try it again. You might even like it. Guaranteed—"Harry" will.

I have never seen
a U-Haul
attached to
a hearse.

In his book, *Ordering Your Private World*, Gordon MacDonald makes the distinction between people who are "driven" and people who are "called." Driven people spend most of their time defending what they own—their ideas, relationships, possessions, etc.

On the other hand, called people live by the philosophy that everything is on loan. They contend that we come into this world with nothing, and we leave with nothing. I agree, with one exception. I think when all is said and done, all we can take with us is the love we feel toward others and the love they have sent our way.

Rabbi Harold Kushner, author of *When Bad Things Happen to Good People*, said: "I've never heard someone on their deathbed say, 'I wish I'd gone to the office more!' They all say something like, 'I wish I'd cared more. I wish I'd loved more. I wish I'd reached out to others more.'" It is both a sobering thought and a call to action.

Inquire within.

M ost of the significant advances in human history—great social and political reformations, artistic productions, unique inventions, etc.—have come not from rushing around but from being still. They required periods of deep and rigorous contemplation, for only in this way can we escape the clamor of outer voices that remind us of "how we've always done it."

How do we find this time for solitude and introspection? We must stake it out for ourselves. One top manager I know does not allow his people to talk on the phone or meet between 8:30 and 9:30 in the morning. This is their quiet time. I used to talk to people on airplanes. Now I use that time to reflect, read, write, or just quiet my mind. I am amazed by my creativity after a long flight.

The point here is that there is no way to do silence wrong. The only thing "wrong" would be not to do it.

People in
organizations
need to develop
a fascination
for what
doesn't work.

When a mistake is made in your organization, what's the first question asked? "What can we learn?" or "Who is to blame?" Most leaders continue to adhere to the old unwritten rule that admonishes them to cover up errors and hide mistakes.

The tendency is to move from crisis to crisis, hardly stopping to see what went wrong. This leads to denial and causes us to look away from errors rather than toward them— kind of like a golfer who hits a bad drive and doesn't want to watch as it heads for the woods.

A few forward-thinking companies have learned to celebrate mistakes as opportunities for learning. I know of a large organization that shoots off a cannon when a big mistake is made. They're not saying they enjoy making errors; they're saying it's time for everyone to learn something. Other organizations would do well to adopt a similar policy. After all, how can they improve if they don't learn from their mistakes?

Choose work you
love and
you will never
have to work a day
in your life.

Confucius

For most people, there's a big difference between work and play. Work is something you have to do; play is something you choose to do. I believe the greatest job is when you can't tell the difference, and the best leaders are those who absolutely love what they're doing.

Don Shula was a great football coach because there was nothing he'd rather be doing on a Sunday than coaching his team toward victory.

To ensure that your work is also your play, I recommend that you develop a personal mission statement. This will help you find what it is you enjoy so much that you lose track of time when you're doing it. That's a difficult concept for some people. But why shouldn't life be about doing what you love? If you don't enjoy what you're doing, how can you be really good at it?

We should all be saying, "Thank God, it's Monday!"

Winning coaches
make their teams
audible-ready.

Ken Blanchard and Don Shula
Everyone's a Coach

An "audible" is a football term—a verbal command used to alert the players to substitute new assignments for the ones they were prepared to perform. Suppose for example, that the quarterback goes to the line of scrimmage and realizes that the defense has figured out their strategy and is ready to stop them. Does he follow through with the doomed play? Of course not. He signals for a different play that has a better chance of success. An audible allows the quarterback to do *what makes sense.*

Audibles are not just last-minute orders the quarterback has dreamed up out of nowhere. These are strategies that players know about and have practiced. There is nothing wrong with plans, or policies, or rules. The problem comes when people are told to implement them no matter what.

I get frustrated with people who tell customers, "Sorry, that's our policy" even when the policy doesn't make sense. Teach your people to bring their brains to work and be "audible-ready."

Never
punish
a learner.

Ken Blanchard and Spencer Johnson
The One Minute Manager®

A friend of mine called me about house training his new dog. "When he has an accident on the rug," he told me, "I plan to shove his nose in it, pound him on the butt with a newspaper, and throw him out the kitchen window into the backyard." How do you think that will work?

I laughed because I knew what would happen. After three days of this treatment, the dog would poop on the floor and jump out the window! That's the kind of confusion you will get when you use punishment on a learner who lacks confidence or may not yet be clear on what you want from him or her. I suggest redirection.

When a learner makes a mistake, be sure that he or she knows immediately that the behavior was incorrect. Place the blame on yourself by saying, "Sorry, I didn't make it clear." Then patiently redirect by reviewing the assignment. If possible, demonstrate what a good job looks like. Observe the learner's new behavior in the hope of catching him or her doing something approximately right and praising progress.

People are okay, it's their behavior that's a problem sometimes.

Ken Blanchard and Spencer Johnson
The One Minute Manager®

What's the best response when one of your people makes a mistake? First of all, check out the facts. If the person admits the mistake and corrects it, you're off the hook. If not, I recommend the "One Minute Reprimand."

Tell the person involved exactly what he or she did wrong and how it impacted the team or organization. Next, share with the person how you feel about it ("I'm frustrated and disappointed with what happened"). Pause for a moment to let your remarks sink in and then reaffirm your confidence in the individual.

People sometimes ask, "Why reaffirm someone you're upset with?" Reaffirming is important, because you want the person to walk away thinking about correcting the wrong behavior rather than how he or she has been mistreated or misunderstood. You want to get rid of the behavior rather than the person.

Consistency isn't behaving the same way all the time.

Ken Blanchard and Don Shula
Everyone's a Coach

Consistency does not mean behaving the same way *all the time.* It actually means behaving the same way *under similar circumstances.* I believe in praising people, but I also know that if you praise them when they are performing well and also when they are performing poorly, you are sending them an inconsistent message. Good performance should always be treated differently than poor performance.

Many leaders make the mistake of letting their mood determine how they respond to their people. If they're feeling great, they wander around praising everyone. If they're feeling lousy, they wander around pointing out what everyone is doing wrong.

When you respond to your people in the same way *under similar circumstances,* you give them a valuable gift—the gift of predictability. There are many ways to inspire good performance but what maintains and improves it is responding consistently.

This is the first time
in the history of
business that you
can be great at
what you're doing
today and be
out of business
tomorrow.

Ken Blanchard and Terry Waghorn
Mission Possible

Constant change is a way of life in business today. In fact, to stay competitive, you must simultaneously manage the present and plan the future.

The problem is, you can't have the same people doing both jobs. If people with present-time operational responsibilities are asked to think about the future, they will kill it. If people with responsibilities for the future also have present-time duties, the urgent problems of today will drag them away from tomorrow's opportunities.

My wife, Margie, recently stepped down as president of our company to become Director of the Office of the Future. She has a four-member team, which has been freed from present-time responsibilities in order to focus all their attention on future trends and technology changes in our industry. The team proposes to the board of directors any changes they see need to be made. The board weighs the merits of the proposal and decides whether to pass it on to the present-time leaders. Once a future sighting is turned over to the present-time leaders, the office of the future lets go of it.

The only
job security
you have today is
your commitment
to continuous
personal
improvement.

When I graduated from college, a friend of mine got a job with AT&T. He called home to tell his mother, and she cried, "You're set for life." Are you set for life with AT&T today? Of course not, and neither are you set for life with any other organization. The "Old Deal" (loyalty in exchange for job security) is over.

In searching for the "New Deal," I've asked people all over the world, "If you can't have job security, what do you want from an organization?" First of all, they want honesty. Secondly, they want the opportunity to learn new skills. If they have to look for a new job, internally or externally, they want to be able to compete.

Once you realize the reality of the "New Deal," you must make up your mind to control your circumstances by means of continuous personal improvement. The sign on your bathroom mirror should say, *Getting better all the time.*

When you
know what you
stand for,
you can turn
around on
a dime and have
five cents change.

Ask yourself how long it would take your people to process a major product change, get behind it, and still meet deadlines. The key to an outstanding, enthusiastic, flexible, and on-time team is to make sure your people are values-driven, rather than goals-driven. If the number one shared value is to serve the customer, then they will be ready to do whatever it takes to live that value.

Sheldon Bowles and I, in our book *Gung Ho!*, make an important distinction between values and goals. The minute you proclaim a goal, it's real, it's set. Values don't work that way. Values become real only when you demonstrate them in the way you act and the way you insist others behave. Goals are for the future; values are for now. Goals are set; values are lived. Goals change; values are rocks you can count on.

Share the cash, then share the congratulations.

Ken Blanchard and Sheldon Bowles
Gung Ho!

You can pat your people on the back and congratulate them all you want, but if you're not taking care of their need for cash, these praisings won't ring true.

I was working with a major retail chain which was experiencing an annual turnover rate of more than 100 percent. The odd thing was that an up-to-date employee opinion survey showed that the workers liked the company, approved of the way they were being managed, and appreciated the upbeat environment. "Why are they leaving when we get such positive feedback?" the chairman asked me. "Did you notice that the lowest ranked survey item was pay and benefits?" I asked. "People are leaving because their basic needs are not being met."

A large segment of our U.S. population is hurting financially. So remember, if you want to build credibility, the rule is: *First* cash, *then* congratulations.

There is no pillow as soft as a clear conscience.

John Wooden

In today's competitive environment, some leaders are tempted to abandon ethical considerations. Somehow they think that playing by the rule of "anything goes" is going to win for them.

These leaders are jeopardizing far more than they imagine. First of all, they stand to lose respect. The number one characteristic employees say they are looking for in a leader is integrity. They also risk losing repeat customers and competent people. You can make a quick financial gain by taking advantage of your customers or your people, but the loss of trust may never be restored. The third thing they are placing at risk is their own self-esteem.

Yes, self-esteem! Meeting people with a clear conscience puts you at ease and allows you to concentrate on doing your best work. When you deal straight with people, they sense that they can trust you. And when you lie down at night, your clear conscience makes a wonderfully soft pillow.

It's surprising
how much you
can accomplish
if you don't
care who gets
the credit.

Abraham Lincoln

It is healthy and justified to feel good about your accomplishments. That's what "true" pride is all about. But there is a "false" pride that distorts people's images of their own importance. They think they deserve *all* the credit, are the source of *all* ideas, and *their* work is the most important. Nothing can get leaders off track more quickly than a "big head" and false pride.

Sharing credit is all about self-esteem. People who have to get all the credit and act like they are the only ones who count are actually covering up their own "I-don't-count" feelings.

Suppose tomorrow you are struck by a lightning bolt that increases your self-esteem by 100 percent. Would you act differently? Sure you would. Would you be willing to share credit with your people? Of course. Would they perform better as a result? You had better believe it. Let's hope for some lightning bolts!

Positive thinkers
get positive results
because they
are not afraid
of problems.

Ken Blanchard and
Norman Vincent Peale
The Power of Ethical Management

I know the minute you mention the word "problem" the implication is that you are speaking negatively. But some don't see it that way.

People often asked Norman Vincent Peale, "Don't you think life would be better if we had fewer problems?" Norman would answer that question by saying, "I'll be happy to take you to Woodlawn Cemetery because the only people I know who don't have any problems are dead."

Norman felt it was possible that the more problems you have, the more alive you were. "If you have no problems at all," he would say, "you're in grave jeopardy!" In fact, if you really insisted that you had no problems, he would suggest that you immediately race home, go straight to your bedroom and slam the door. Then get down on your knees and pray: "What's the matter, Lord? Don't You trust me anymore? Give me some problems!"

Early in life, people
give up their health
to *gain* wealth. . . .
In later life, people
give up some of
their wealth
to *regain* health!

Ken Blanchard, D. W. Edington,
and Marjorie Blanchard
*The One Minute Manager®
Balances Life and Work*

If you don't watch out, success can kill you. When *The One Minute Manager®* leaped onto the best-seller list, I found myself running around the country giving speeches, conducting interviews on radio and TV—doing all the things that seem to come with material success.

One day I looked at myself and realized I was overweight, not exercising, sleep deprived, and generally treating my body like it was indestructible. My wife, Margie, was telling me I needed to get my life in balance. Finally, I took the advice of my wife and friends and began to develop a sensible lifestyle program. It was then that Dee Edington, Margie, and I began writing *The One Minute Manager® Balances Life and Work* (formerly *The One Minute Manager® Gets Fit*). By the time the book came off the press, I was the picture of health.

The reality was, I needed that book more than anyone else. I had to give up some of my wealth to regain my health. What are you doing?

Servant leadership
is more about
character
than style.

In his book, *Servant Leadership*, Robert Greenleaf defines two kinds of leaders. Strong *natural leaders* are those who try to take control, make the decisions, and give the orders in any situation in which they find themselves. They have a need to be in charge. Strong *natural servants*, on the other hand, will assume leadership only if they see it as a way in which they can serve.

You would think that natural leaders would use a directive, autocratic style while natural servants would use a more supportive, participative style. This assumption falls short because it confuses style with character.

I want to be led by strong *natural servants* because they are willing to use whatever leadership style—directive, supportive, or some combination—best serves the needs of those they lead. Remember that the primary biblical image of servant leadership is that of the shepherd, because the flock is not there for the sake of the shepherd; the shepherd is there for the sake of the flock.

Ducks quack.
Eagles soar.

Years ago, Wayne Dyer said, "There are two kinds of people in this world: ducks and eagles." Ducks quack a lot and make all kinds of noise. Eagles go about their business and soar above the crowd. You can tell a lot about an organization when you have a customer problem. That's usually when ducks and eagles appear.

Eagles flourish in organizations where the customer is the focus, while ducks multiply in places where boss-pleasing and policy-following carry the day. Let me give you an example.

I once tried to rent a car in Ithaca, New York. I planned to fly out of Syracuse, so I asked for a car *from* Syracuse in order to avoid the drop-off fee. The clerk located a car from Syracuse but the $50 fee remained on my contract. "I can't take it off; my computer won't let me and my boss would kill me," she quacked. It took me twenty minutes to get this woman to remove the drop-off fee. What kind of organization do you think she works for?

Eagles flourish
when
they're free
to fly.

I was greeted the minute I walked into the DMV to replace my lost driver's license. "Welcome. Do you speak English or Spanish?" a woman employee asked. She then ushered me to a counter where a smiling young man asked how he could help me. Nine minutes later, I had a temporary license.

"This isn't the DMV I used to know and love," I commented. "What happened?"

"Haven't you met our manager?" she asked, pointing at a desk smack in the middle of the big room. I walked over to meet "the boss" and found him to be anything but. He told me that it was his job "to reorganize the department on a moment-by-moment basis, depending on customer needs." His commitment to take care of citizens was obvious.

Duck busting was that manager's way of life. He wanted eagles who would create *Raving Fan*® customers. I certainly went away from there as one.

Take responsibility for making relationships work.

L et me ask you a question—the same question you should be asking yourself, not only about your love relationship but also your relationship with your children, your boss, your co-workers, your direct reports, and your friends. *Do you want the relationship to work?* If so, then you must take personal responsibility for making it work. And forget the word "trying." Trying is just a noisier way of *not* doing something.

I know two people who have been married for twenty-five years. They are an inspiration to others. They seem to be courting each other all the time. Whenever they see each other, both light up with joy. It's obvious that they're best friends. It's easy to accentuate the negative, but these two do everything they can to point out the positive and bring out the best in each other. They are both committed to doing whatever it takes to show respect and unconditional appreciation.

In short, they are committed to making their relationship work. That's what it takes these days in all types of relationships.

New today,
obsolete
tomorrow.

It used to be that managers were people who were the best at doing what the people they were supervising did. But things are happening so quickly today that it's almost impossible to be a "know-it-all" anymore. These days, within a year, most managers know far less than their people about what they do. Not admitting this can lead to real problems. Yet traditionally, managers have not been willing to share their vulnerability.

One of the most ingratiating things you can do with your people is to admit your ignorance or vulnerability. Once done, this opens the door for others to share their expertise, and for you to become a cheerleader, supporter, and encourager.

We're all sometimes confused, lost, or afraid. If we come clean about it, we create trust and empower others to learn and grow. So if you're obsolete, who cares? Someone around you will have the answer, and your ignorance will allow them to shine.

G.O.L.F.
stands for
Game of Life First.

Ken Blanchard
The One Minute Golfer
(formerly *Playing the Great Game of Golf*)

I've often said I can find out more about someone during one round of golf than by working with them for a long period of time. Like life, golf is a game where you get some good breaks and some bad breaks you *don't* deserve, and some good breaks and bad breaks you *do* deserve.

In most sports, you are reacting to someone else, but in golf you are reacting to your own performance. Sometimes you are playing better than you expect and dealing with success; sometimes you are playing worse than you expect and dealing with failure.

Golf brings out the best and worst in people. If you cheat or blow up when you have a bad break, that same behavior will show up in other parts of your life. If you maintain a positive attitude when things go sour, that will carry over into other things also. What better training ground is there for learning to accept the bitter with the sweet, than the golf course? Go ahead! Tee it up!

Leadership is not
something you
do *to* people.
It's something you
do *with* people.

Ken Blanchard, Patricia Zigarmi,
and Drea Zigarmi
Leadership and The One Minute Manager®

When we first started teaching Situational Leadership® II, we found that leaders got excited about it and started using the concepts with their people. The only problem was, they didn't tell anybody. As a result, people got confused, even when they were using the concepts well.

For example, suppose you have found some of your employees to be self-reliant achievers. Because you feel they can work well with little supervision, you stop going by to see them. Suppose also that you have several enthusiastic beginners who need to be told how and why to do things. The achievers might feel undervalued and overlooked, while the beginners could feel you are picking on them.

When you share your leadership strategy with your people, they not only understand what you have in mind but they can give you helpful feedback. True servant leaders want feedback because they are anxious to know whether their interactions with their people are helpful and effective. So don't do leadership *to* people, do it *with* them.

Don't settle for less than a Fortun*ate* 500 company.

Ken Blanchard and Michael O'Connor
Managing by Values®

What is a Fortun*ate* 500 Company? It's an organization that has:

1) Motivated customers who keep coming back;
2) Inspired employees who give their best each day;
3) Owners who enjoy profits made in an ethically fair manner;
4) Significant others (suppliers, community, vendors, distributors, and even respected competitors) who thrive on the mutual trust and respect they feel toward the company.

How do you get relationships like that? It's the result of MBV—Managing By Values. There are three MBV steps: identifying core values, communicating core values, and aligning values and practice. All are important.

Take time to identify core values.

I dentifying the core values that define your organization is one of the most important functions of leadership. The success or failure of this process can literally make or break an organization.

For example, let's look at Disney. This organization has identified four values for its theme parks. They are safety, courtesy, the show (being in role, whether it's being Mickey Mouse or a ticket taker), and efficiency. Not only have they identified their values but they have also carefully ordered them. Why is this important? A bottom-line oriented manager might emphasize efficiency and thus jeopardize the other three values.

You would be wise to make the identification of your organization's core values a top priority. And don't try to do this job alone. Take advantage of the resources you have around you. Draw in your people—everyone should have ownership in this process. Remember that rules can be imposed but values cannot. Bring everyone into the process early.

Core values

must be

communicated.

Identifying your organization's core values is a worthless exercise unless those values are constantly communicated and your people and customers see that you are completely committed to them.

In fact, it's impossible to affirm them too much. Talk about your organization's values; put them on your business cards, annual reports, plaques, wall signs, and job aids. In short, display them anywhere your people, customers, stockholders, and significant others can see them.

You must give more than lip service to these values. However, lip service is an important step in the process. Stating and restating until they become second nature breeds security for your people and your customers alike. They will begin to know what to expect from your organization, and that kind of recognition will set you apart from the crowd.

Walk your talk.

Without some method of locating gaps between values and behavior, identifying and communicating core values will do more harm than good. An organization that talks about putting the customer first, for example, but fails to do so, is far more likely to be judged harshly by its people and customers alike.

This means that it is vital for organizations and their leadership to "walk their talk." They must make every effort to become living symbols of their organization's value system. This is simple common sense. Eighty percent of the time allocated for implementing the "Managing By Values®" process is given to this step. Why? Because without it, the other steps are useless.

The good news is that once core values have been set in place—identified, communicated, and impacting behavior— they become the "boss." Just remember though, this is an ongoing process—a journey without a finish line.

Knowing where you're going is the first step to getting there.

Ken Blanchard
We Are the Beloved

Have you identified your mission in life—your reason for being? Establishing a *personal mission statement* is an important exercise that has helped me define who I am, identify my priorities, and keep my perspective on target. It involves identifying your passions.

I've noticed that I'm happiest and at my best when I'm teaching or writing. I also want to make a difference in other people's lives. Therefore my mission statement reads: *To be a loving teacher and example of simple truths that help myself and others to awaken the presence of God in our lives.* I say "awaken the presence of God" because I am constantly encouraging myself and others to get our egos out of the way so God can do His work. Remember "EGO" really stands for "Edging God Out."

Look inside yourself and let God help you find the driving force in your life. Doing so is the first step to a happier and more satisfied you.

As a leader, the
most important
earthly relationship
you can cultivate is
your relationship
with yourself.

Ken Blanchard and Terry Waghorn
Mission Possible

Do you really know yourself? Do you have a personal "mission statement" that defines your strengths and motivates you to be all God meant you to be?

If you have trouble with that question, you might want to try an interesting activity that will almost certainly help you develop a clearer sense of purpose and personal identity: *Write your own obituary.*

I know it sounds strange—even a little morbid. But this exercise is not about dying; it's about living. It will give you an opportunity to adjust your life, describe the ideal you, and define what it is you would like to be remembered for. Why leave such important matters to chance? God has a wonderful plan for your life. Let Him help you establish your path and guide you as you walk in it. Nothing will be beyond your reach.

Purpose can never be about achievement; it is much bigger.

Ken Blanchard and Terry Waghorn
Mission Possible

The beauty of writing your own obituary before you die is that it serves as a dream—a big picture of what you want your life to be and mean. So, if you don't like the way your life is shaping up right now, change it. Don't hold back!

Put aside your lesser self and go with your best self. That will probably require some personal meditation, but it will pay big dividends. And reject the lie that says such thinking is egotistical. God made you and He has always intended for you to be the best that you can be. He not only approves, but I have found that He is willing and able to help in your search for self-discovery. Quiet yourself, pray, and listen to the voice that says, "You are loved, richly and unconditionally."

And as you begin, remember that every journey begins with a single step and moves along one step at a time. Enjoy the trip!

Purpose has to do with one's calling—deciding what business you are in as a person.

Ken Blanchard and Norman Vincent Peale
The Power of Ethical Management

I once heard a story about Alfred Nobel, the originator of the Nobel Peace Prize. When his brother died, Nobel got a copy of the newspaper to see what was said about his brother. He was shocked to discover that a dreadful error had been made. The paper had confused him with his brother and the obituary he was reading was his own.

As a young man, Alfred Nobel had been involved in the invention of dynamite, and his premature obituary elaborated on the terrible death and destruction this powerful force had brought into the world. Nobel was devastated. He wanted to be known as a man of "peace." He quickly realized that if his obituary was to be rewritten, he would have to do it himself by changing the nature of his life. So Alfred Nobel did just that. I dare say that Alfred Nobel is better known today for his contribution to peace rather than for any other thing he did in his life.

Your life is yours to design. Make it all it can be!

About the Author

Ken Blanchard has impacted the day-to-day management of people and companies around the world as a prominent, gregarious, sought-after author, speaker, and business consultant. A polished storyteller with a knack for making the seemingly complex easy to understand, he is universally characterized as one of the most insightful, powerful, and compassionate men in business today.

Ken's best-selling book, *The One Minute Manager,* co-authored with Spencer Johnson, has sold more than nine million copies worldwide. His books *Raving Fans* and *Gung Ho!* (both with Sheldon Bowles) are also major best-sellers along with five other books in *The One Minute Manager Library.*

Ken is the chief spiritual officer of The Ken Blanchard Companies, a group of companies in the management training and consulting business that he and his wife, Dr. Marjorie Blanchard, founded in 1979. He is also visiting lecturer at his alma mater, Cornell University, where he received his B.A. and Ph.D. degrees and is a trustee emeritus of the board of trustees.

For more information about Ken Blanchard's books, speeches, and consulting, contact:

The Ken Blanchard Companies
125 State Place
Escondido, California 92029
or call:
1-800-728-6000
or visit:
www.blanchardtraining.com